Amazing Grace

Larry D. Thomas

Texas Review Press
Huntsville, Texas

FIRST EDITION, 2001

Requests for permission to reproduce material from this work should be sent
to:

Permissions
Texas Review Press
English Department
Sam Houston State University
Huntsville, TX 77341-2146

Cover design by Paul Ruffin
Cover art ("Prickly Pear") by Lisa P. Thomas

ACKNOWLEDGMENTS

The author offers grateful acknowledgment to the editors of the following
periodicals in which many of the poems herein were originally published,
sometimes in slightly different versions:

*Blue Violin, Borderlands: Texas Poetry Review, Cape Rock, The Chattahoo-
chee Review, Concho River Review, DeKalb Literary Arts Journal, Descant,
Desert Candle, Green Hills Literary Lantern, Louisiana Literature, Maverick
Press, Midwest Quarterly, Poet Lore, Poetry Depth Quarterly, Puerto del Sol,
RE:AL, Rio Grande Review, Southwest Review, Southwestern American
Literature, Spoon River Poetry Review, Sulphur River Literary Review, Texas
Probation: The Journal of the Texas Probation Association, Texas Review,
Webster Review, Writers' Forum*

"Of Eyes Wondrously Wild" also appeared in the 1997 edition of the *Antho-
logy of Magazine Verse & Yearbook of American Poetry.*

"Mooring Line" first appeared in *The Lighthouse Keeper*, a collection of
poems issued by Timberline Press.

Library of Congress Cataloging-in-Publication Data

Thomas, Larry, 1947-
    Amazing Grace / Larry D. Thomas.-- 1st ed.
        p. cm.
    ISBN 1-881515-40-0 (alk. paper)
    I. Title

PS3620.H63 A43 2001
811'.6--dc21   2001052286

for my daughter, Deena

CONTENTS

I. Their Heaven of Bleakness

II. Near the Big Thicket

III. At the Jetty's End

IV. A Short Distance from the Border

I.

Their Heaven of Bleakness

"Of Dust Thou Art"

In Van Horn, in far West Texas,
the sun has turned their faces
into deep red leathery brains.
They breathe dry air laden with red earth,

their lungs the lower halves
of rubbery hourglasses
turning year by sedulous year,
right before their eyes, into dust.

Even the hard oaken pews
they sit on during worship are dust-filmed
where they wheeze with clotted breath
the strains of "Amazing Grace."

Evenings, after the sun
has wobbled like a glob
down the rock-and-cactus-fleshed slopes
of mountains their forebears named "Diablo,"

they take to their gritty beds,
ease the quilts of grandmas
over their leathery bodies
like slabs of red earth, and they pray.

Herefords in Winter

It's nine degrees above zero.
They stand still in the pasture, staring
at nothing but the barbs of taut wire,

the sky above them so blue and cold
that even the hawks have taken shelter.
They stare chewing their cud

against a distant backdrop of cap rock
their white faces hover over
like full, haunting moons familiar with sky

and the feeble daily scaldings
of the sun. They stare straight through
their barbed and lone existences,

surviving the cold,
flourishing in their heaven
of bleakness.

The Wind

At night,
after dry winters,
under patterned quilts
oozing the cedar
of the chests
of dead relatives,
parents dream of it
ripping tumbleweeds
from their roots
to roam forever
like ghosts
of the troubled dead.
They dream
of their children
leaning into it
with stinging eyes,
crawling to get home,
struggling to breathe
through bright
red kerchiefs
tied behind
their heads.
They dream
of its howling
as it tears
through the bright
red threads,
already filling
the little lungs
of their heirs
with the rich
red fields
of deep lineage.

The Red Raging Waters

For weeks on end it has rained in Texas
Sending the Brazos miles beyond its banks
Where it rises even now under dark Texas skies

Over the wooden floor of a bottomland Baptist church,
Floating creaking pews shaped with the aching buttocks
Of generations, the wild Brazos rising higher yet

To the stained-glass robes of the Apostles,
Soaking the feet of Jesus and lapping the elbows
Of His uplifted arms, creeping up the pulpit

On whose open Bible coils a fat diamondback,
The red raging waters of the Brazos
Bringing to sweet communion the serpent and the saint.

Mesquite Carver

It so pervades their decades,
to keep it from taking over
their pastures, the ranchers
attack it with chain saws
whose teeth it smoothes to gum,
rip out its stumps with tractors,
and pile it high for burning.

Though it chisels
more like marble than wood,
she chooses it for its grain,
burls and deep red hue
the color of dried blood.
She fights it into hawk,
prickly pear, scorpion,

rattler and the busts
of her three dead husbands,
her ubiquitous,
indomitable medium,
obdurate almost
as the lives to which
it bears such eerie likeness.

Palo Duro Canyon

A straight
razor,
this wind
of winter

scraping
high plains
till they bleed,
scraping

toward a canyon
where cedar clings
to sheer faces
of cliffs,

clawing roots
into hard
red scabs
of earth,

this wind
of winter
scraping its way
to a canyon rim

where hawks,
slingshot-flung,
scream in dazzling
Texas sun.

High Cotton

Under mesquite branches
gnarled as the interlocked,
arthritic fingers of our grandmas,
she spread our blanket
on dunes of sand
violate with tracks of horned frogs.

She lay on her back in the shade,
winked, and showed me
her pink cotton panties.
The noon sun dappled her flesh
with patches of brilliant light.
I lay beside her terrified

but feigning manliness
as if I could have handled
the budding turbulence of her lust.
I lay beside her fumbling
at my crumpled Levi's fly,
saved by the blessed fluke

of my new Fruit of the Looms
catching ever so graciously
in the bright copper teeth of my zipper
gleaming its broad Texas grin
that summer I was seven
and she had just turned ten.

Dust Storm

The West Texas sky
at high noon,
turning to nothing
but loose red land
one with wind.
The horses,
looming in the pasture

like bodies
of the drowned
suspended in fathoms
of swirling,
blood-colored earth,
each horse a monument
of composure

tilting a back hoof
in perfect calm
though slowly
being buried alive,
turning to dust
right before the eyes
of the rider.

For Purity

for Georgia O'Keeffe

she dons jet-black
and takes her stance
before the canvas,

draping her heart
with the shadow
of a black cross.

She scours her mind
with cloudless
desert sky

and she waits
for the moon-like rising
of the flower,

the pelvis,
the cleansed,
sun-bleached skull.

Warrior Woman

At night
among the ancient kachinas
in the tomb-like silence
of the museum
looms this dark little doll

of pure spirit
carved of cottonwood root
with a flake of stone,
painted with a brush
of stiff yucca fiber.

Her face is black,
her mouth a rectangle
lined in red,
filled with six triangles
of sharp white teeth.

For hundreds of years
she has stood rock-still,
staring down the darkness
with the bright yellow circles
of her eyes.

String Cadenza

The cowhand's
Sun and ice-lined face,

Its features
Harsh and sharpened
Like a wind-hewn peak,

Reeks of half-cooked
Barbecued brisket.

His fingers are stiff
From castrating calves
In the cold,

His legs bowed
To the great rib cage
Of a quarter horse

Whose savage hairs
String the bows of violins.

The Stringer

for Roy L. Thomas and Samuel E. Thomas

We caught but a single perch
that morning on Oak Creek Lake,
threaded the stringer through its gills,
and lowered it back to the depths

from which it came. We were calm,
the surface of the lake was perfectly smooth,
and our live bait writhing on our hooks
was, we thought, the only thing moving.

Little did we know that beneath us
the perch was already half-engorged
by a cottonmouth, engaged
in a futile struggle for its life.

We just kept fishing, floating
calmly on the surface of things,
the stringer taut at our boat's side,
chaining us to the unforgiving darkness.

Bus Hand

in memory of Roy Lee Thomas

The light that morning, trickling from a single bulb,
was dim as my wisdom in his kitchen where,
hunched over cups of black coffee and across
the plastic-topped dinette table from one another,
Dad and I sat, just months before he died.

After a while, with neither of us having much to say,
he placed his right hand at the center of the table
and asked me to do likewise. His hand could have passed
for van Gogh's peasant's shoe, its leathery flesh
creased with decades of manual labor,

so lined with dirty oil from his service station
that even a fierce scrubbing with a bar of Lava soap
couldn't clean it. Though mute, it mumbled a thousand stories.
Mine, in embarrassing contrast, was soft and smooth
as a lady's, taxed with but the handle of a briefcase.

He then asked if I knew what our hands were, paused
and said his was a bus hand, mine a plane.
Said when he traveled, if he had to, it was by bus;
I, by plane. As he stared at me, I noticed how
even the hardly managed line of his smile was jagged.

Primary Colors

for Deena, in memory of Edith Coleman Thomas

For several months,
Mom's clinical depression
had kept her indoors.
She killed time
drifting through her universe

of drugs, clad
in but her gown
and pale blue housecoat
she kept buttoning
below her knees for prudence.

One late October day,
after a blue norther
had passed through town,
rubbing the sky
to raw cobalt,

my daughter of three
led her by her pinkie
to the backyard,
got her to lie down
in the grass

and buried
all but the cameo
of her face
under a foot or more
of red and yellow leaves,

believing
with all her heart
that that many reds and yellows
couldn't help but thaw her
grandma's blues.

For Reasons All Their Own

The same water
the windmill used to promise
has left it in a shroud of rust,
both it and the roof

of the old vacant farmhouse
whose windows gape
like toothless mouths.
For reasons all their own

little children keep meeting there
and lie near the rock fireplace,
their downy cheeks rosed by the heat
of a make-believe fire.

They keep meeting there
to hide from their parents
their roles, their dead-serious roles
of a grown-up farmer and his farmwife.

His little arm's
tightening around her shoulders now
as she shudders to the screams
of dead women.

Just a few feet above them
the screams, the muffled screams
of each savage, bygone birthing
keep creaking in the dark rafters.

Claret Cup Cactus

In the Trans-Pecos,
near Williams Ranch
on the wind-razed flanks
of the Guadalupe Mountains,

it flourishes in its garden
not of Eden but of rocks,
of arroyos gouged
by torrents of rarest rain

and punished mercilessly
by the sun, enduring
in desiccated air
saline from salt flats

miles away, ever so close
to shade thrown by creosote
and ocotillo shimmering
just short of its blistered flesh,

enduring another April
and, as if pricked
by its own star-shaped thorns,
blooming blood.

Rattlesnake Roundup

At sunrise bands of gunless hunters
Stud the bleak, West Texas landscape,
Clutching forked sticks, wide-eyed at openings
Of cap rock dens, shoving vees

Behind the venom-bulged heads of vipers,
Bagging their catch in coarse tow sacks
For the trip to the town coliseum,
To pits teeming with fugues of fierce rattling

Where handlers press fangs against lips of jars,
Milking poison, and butchers section cuts
For deep fryers, cooking sweet, snow-white meat
For the leathery mouths of old townsfolk.

Turkey Vultures

At sundown our first day on the campground
we saw them across Inks Lake,
roosting in the branches of a dead tree,

their black silhouettes looming, absolutely still
against a backdrop of blinding orange.
We wondered if they were eagles.

They didn't come closer till the day we left,
daringly close, scavenging our neighbors'
deserted campsite, sparring on the ground

for a single, fetid shred of charred chicken.
As we walked toward them they fluttered
to the tops of ancient trees,

their heads gracefully drooped,
their red, wrinkled flesh pulled taut over their skulls
like the hoods of executioners.

As we walked closer they took to the sky,
rowing their bodies through the mist
with the lithe black oars of their wings,

gliding in high circles above us,
biding their time in the brief,
tenuous eddies of our lives.

Amazing Grace

As both generations of the blood kin before her,
Grace has lived her life on her grandfather's spread.
She's never cared as much for the townsfolk
as the barren majesty of the land itself.
She's never even thought about leaving.
It's as if she herself were fashioned from its clay,
eased by a shovel from her mother's womb

and blessed some way with the miracle of breath.
In her withered spinsterhood, long retired
from her forty years of teaching high school English,
she still rises before first light
and takes her place in her porch rocker.
When moonless, her night sky's a black velvet
jeweler's cloth of roiling solitaires.

Among the adults of her West Texas hamlet,
she's lived her life a closet sophisticate,
just to keep down trouble. Perhaps that's why
she rises every day before dawn for the breaking
of light so intense it's palpable; warm, amber light
savory as the brandy of aged literature
swirling in the snifter of her skull.

"And to Dust Thou Shalt Return"

In a far West Texas hamlet,
the winter night is moonless,
blueblack as the plumes of crows.

Of adobe a house of worship's
wedged in a small canyon
at the base of the Davis Mountains.

Atop its crude belfry, anchored
in a socket of straw and dried mud,
a solitary white cross

shines with starlight and creaks
under a glaze of clear blue ice.
Inside the sanctuary

looming in the night like an ember
crunched by a boot into a cranny
of rocky ground, shackled

as if with granite, yet glowing,
the thin worshipers, their desiccated
bodies but joyous skeletons

dancing under hides of dust,
crumble the clods of old voices
into song.

II

Near the Big Thicket

Fox Fire

After weeks of light rain
the floor of the woods
is sodden as a bog,

a patchwork of oxblood
and mustard tallow leaves
disintegrating from the thread-

like skeletons of their veins
in the black machinations
of rot, scat-scented,

shining with frog-slime, upthrust
by the shoots of mushrooms
muscling their way through the mire,

loosing old fox-stink
to slither through the mist
like warm steam.

The Slough

The decaying pine boards of his porch
creak beneath the rockers of stained oak
shaped by the hands of his father.
He kills his time there, rocking,

staring deep into the woods
of his grandfather, toward the slough.
For ten years, since he turned seventy,
it's risen in the basement of his dreams.

The haven of gator and cottonmouth,
it's harbored for three generations
his clan's deepest secrets. Late at night,
if he listens hard enough, he can hear

the muffled, steady engine of its rot.
It works its timeless wonders
under still, dark waters. Its film
has already claimed his pale, blue eyes.

Lumberjack

His nostrils are caked with resin
scorched by the screaming,
spinning steel of blades.

His dreams are crows
cawing in the crotches
of old-growth pines

sentineling the undisturbed
acres of a virgin forest.
Like his father

and grandfather before him,
the only job he knows
lies in the razor-

sharp teeth of saws
whining through hearts
harder than a whore's.

Even in his sleep
it twitches for the trigger
of a chain saw,

the scar-fleshed,
last surviving finger
of his only hand.

Caddoan Indian Mound

Near Crockett, Texas,
the wind, warm still
after all these years

with the chants of shamans,
whispers through the needles
of pines and eddies

about the beaks of owls.
Tens of feet in height
it rises from the earth

in a breathless
ritual of moonglow,
this mound of pure spirit

ascending the night sky
on its staircase
of sacred skulls.

Crows Roosting

The winter sky is numinous,
overcast with layers of cloud-gauze
wrapped loosely around the luminous
oozing wound of Sunday morning.

The leaves, what few remain
of the Chinese tallow,
have capitulated to a stain
of oxblood, burgundy, and harvest gold,

hanging by their stems for dear life
and an imminent pirouette to death.
Deep within the leaves' tenuous strife
they roost, these priests and priestesses

of darkness, blue-black with blight,
preening the sheen of their plumes,
each a grim reminder of the night
making the morning so terribly bright.

These Blooms

in late
afternoon
so red

they hurt.
These blooms
of the hibiscus.

These wide-
open mouths
of sopranos

bleeding
from singing
the brilliant,

unbroken
high C's
of these full

yet day-
long
lives.

Great Blue Heron

after a painting by Vic Bowen

He stands
flawlessly still
on his spindly,
stilt-like legs
as if an outgrowth

of the rotting,
half-submerged branches
he clutches
with his clawed,
gangly feet

crusted with muck
and the must
of alligator snappers.
He stands
a prince of mire

poised at the brink
of night,
his dagger-beak
stabbed deep
into the blue-

black bowels of twilight,
the fetid, scraggly
feathers of his breast
ablaze with the death throes
of a wobbling sun.

Tumescence

The clouds, protuberant
with the urgency of rain,
sag the gray fabric

of the sky. Her nostrils,
swollen with fluid, flare
with the scent of biscuits

rising in the wood stove.
The slats of her rocker
bow under the heaviness

of imminent birthing.
Her hand, weary from tracing
the aching curvature

of her twelve-pound, past-due son,
dangles near a rosebush
whose burgeoning pinks, poised

as the scalpels of surgeons,
start splitting the drum-
stretched sheaths of their buds,

the possibility
of a Caesarean section
remote as lights, running water.

Of His Presence

A hawk is perched on a telephone wire,
His back to the highway, his black mind

Oblivious of the drone of passing cars.
He faces east where the winter sun

Is rising, rending the firmament
With its beak of fire. He gazes

Over his mired dominion of slough,
His brain a bullet of hot blood,

His frosted talons shuddering
With the drum roll of his blackened heart.

His head bowed forward, vulture-like,
He gazes, fending off the cold,

The brutal cold, with nothing but the hooded,
Brooding terror of his presence.

Late Sonata

For sixty years a teacher of piano
and well into her eighties,
she wakes into the glory

of another spring,
pressing white fingers
deep into dark potting soil

as she plants a geranium
shaking its scarlet fists,
her hearing aid

percussive with the dissonance of jays
dripping through budding oak branches
like pints of spilled blue paint.

As she tamps the damp soil,
her mind turns
to the cool ecstasy of evening

when her fingers will flutter
over a keyboard of wisteria,
seeking choice flowers she'll pluck,

dip in fresh batter,
and fry for a light evening meal
of fragrant lavender.

Fixing the Scene

An indolent
April morning
on the patio

the plants
with hushed tongues
slurping the scalpel light

the lizards
peppering a brick wall
like old green women
sprawled on their bellies
in the sun

the geraniums
fixing the scene

each red petal a note
in the chilling score
of a Hitchcock flick

just before
a murder.

Winter Rye

January with its vengeful hand
chokes the trunk of a Chinese tallow
and shakes it as if in reprimand,

clacking its bare branches against one another
like the antlers of rutting bucks.
January has cast the pallor

of its annual reign over the earth,
though something is there that won't submit
to its dominion, sprouting its mirth

in tufted insurrections of green contrarily
growing lithe thorns deep in the flesh,
the arrogant, leathery flesh of January.

The Azaleas

are waiting
in the shadows
of dangling
Spanish moss

where they're nurtured
year-round
for a moment
of blooming

sudden as light
from a thrown switch.
They're waiting
to flashflood

stately lawns
and stab
the cataracts
of proper

old women
with primitive
profusions
of red.

Mockingbird

In our all too human hubris
we've stuck you with a specious name,
plain bird yet so fiercely territorial
you'll attack a diamondback,
stab its eyes with the dagger of your beak,
and leave it writhing in blindness

to a death by its own venom.
Is it not the other birds which,
stupefied by the virtuosity of your singing,
have stolen but a shred of your cadenza
and made it the sole song of their being?
We just couldn't handle the terrible ease

with which you and you alone
broke each day with a music
so plangent it overshadowed
the breathless pastels of dawn,
so plangent we had to name you
and in our human frailty named you wrong.

We had to rob you of your grand creative prowess
and claim it as our own,
as the only thing which lofted us
above the lesser animals,
so we named you *mocker*,
hoarding *maker* for our false, false selves.

A Sunday Morning

of pure silence,
whose only motion
is the chill of a heavy dew,

is cast in precious metal.
The church garden petunias
plastered to the ground by night rain

are left a used palette,
the leftover oils of a masterpiece,
but the green rosebuds are still intact,

leaning on their stems,
fattening on sunlight
and the nutrients of dark earth,

still as the huge cathedral bells
electric with the violent promise
of ringing.

This Morning in July

on what will be the hottest
day of the year, another dead limb
cracks from the trunk of an old

Chinese tallow, shattering the air
with another clap of thunder.
Shirtless, gloveless, and well into his eighties,

the widower stretches for another limb,
pulls with all his might, and sends another clap
through the morning calm of his Saturday.

Placing his right foot at the big limb's center,
he eases its narrow end toward his torso
and breaks the limb cleanly in half.

His pruning completed with nothing
but his bare hands, he stacks the dead logs
neat as a cord of firewood. He rests,

raking his hands over the bark,
handling his deepening darkness
with the sure natural ease of a master.

Carnations

Within her cloud of clean sheets
spotless as the uniforms of nurses,
unraveling from her eyes

the gauze of difficult sleep,
she sees them on the stainless
steel table beneath the window

of her private room.
She marvels at their radiance,
at how, though amputated

from their feet of roots,
they still stand, propped
on the sturdy green crutches

of their stems; at how,
round as the mouths of a choir,
their perfect blooms

glorify a shaft of sunlight
with the blood-red certitude
of remission.

Of Eyes Wondrously Wild

for Lisa

Clawing the street
under the tree of its birth,
it lay there on asphalt
cooling with shadows of evening.
Limp at its side

hung its broken wing
auguring hidden injuries
ridiculously accidental
and far too soon, fatal.
I eased it with great care

to the cupped left hand
of my wife. With her right
index finger she stroked it
in a futile human attempt
to soothe the dark terrors

of eyes wondrously wild
for the fleeting little seconds
of a life. It blinked
once or twice, shuddered, and died,
her cupped hand its warm coffin.

My wife's eyes watered
and a breeze came,
lifting her hair from her cheeks
like the soft glorious wings
of ascension.

For Bright Candy

The African violets
flourish
on a glass shelf,

root-bound in their shiny
brass pots,
their fleshy leaves twisting

toward the light
like the cupped hands
of little kids

poised for bright candy,
so sensitive
they will rot

from a single drop
of standing water.
They flourish

on a glass shelf,
choking
on their own roots,

gurgling
their rich, deepening
purple.

White Tigresses

Gracing the zoo grounds
Like furred elegant women
Strolling in a winter sun

The little girls waiting, watching them
With squinted blue eyes
Imagining their white pelts

Spread before a fireplace
For the sprawled warm bodies
Of their mothers and strange lovers

Little girls waiting with blue eyes
For the tossed slabs of raw cattle
The thrusts of huge pink tongues

The little girls leaving with their dads,
Falling sound asleep on the back seats
Dreaming of their soft white kittens.

III.

At the Jetty's End

As the Wind Blows

a great storm is building
in the darkness over the Gulf,
waking the elderly and wooing them
in nightclothes to the shoreline
where waves gobble sand
like the huge steel scoops of steam shovels.
The wind blows hard off the Gulf

stripping the elderly of their robes,
plastering loose flesh
against the warm brittle cages of ribs,
pulling back thin silver wisps of hair
like the hands of fierce Comanches
desperate for the scalps of the fallen.
As the wind blows hard off the Gulf,

the elderly keep rising from their beds
and easing seaward, filling old bodies
with the wild, invigorating blasts,
turning weary lungs into the breeze-
swelled canvases of catamarans,
slicing old bodies recklessly
through the dark and raging sea.

The Bathers

After **Bathers**, *c. 1918, by Pablo Picasso*

The Gulf
of molten jade
and whitecaps
is still frigid
with the cold
storage aspect

of winter.
The bathers
are freezing,
wading the hushed
desperation
of their bodies

in the surf,
locked
in the bloody
objects
of heads, trunks,
arms, and legs,

abject,
bone white,
godlike
in but the cold,
abstract eye
of the painter.

Each Color

Ernest bows
in a fugue
of wave and gull

in the stained-glass shade
of catamarans.
Though they are beached

they still sing to him
of gust and wild dance.
He closes his eyes

in the sun
and sees them
slicing seaward

with their men,
their man-made wings,
each color

a vivid,
momentary stay
against the ever.

Of Beasts Become Angels

Freed with the blade
of his pocketknife,
his gulls, skimmers, pelicans,

and great blue herons,
imprisoned for months
in the dark heart

of driftwood, take flight.
He feels the beauty of wings
in wind, of weightless bodies

keeling in the nacreous
liberty of dusk,
and after these moments

of beasts become angels,
braces for descension
to the earthbound,

hard wrought, and dauntless
independence of his chair
on wheels.

Mooring Line

Pearled with barnacles,
it lies half-buried in the dunes
like the necklace of a giant,
flung angrily to the ground.

Braided with thick,
blue and white strands of nylon,
its ends are frazzled
as an old maid's hair, scorched

from one too many permanents.
Its massive size belies its weakness,
its nylon long ago compromised
by sun and weeks on end at sea.

With nothing to show it mercy
but the laggardly deepening sand,
it'll lie this way for months,
sponging the screams and fleeting

shadows of the gulls,
tethering uselessness
to the slow, consuming pull
of ruin.

For Wentletraps

For the fiftieth
straight winter
they breathe
through the virgin wool
of bloodred mufflers

scouring the beach
for tiny
wentletraps,
their blue eyes
a little dimmer

yet focusing
adroitly
through deepening
lenses,
the dull gleam

of delicate
wedding rings
thinning under thick
bright mittens,
the hushed

incipience
of death
toted gently
on their shoulders
like drowsy

great-grandchildren.

Still Water

Once I saw the Gulf
flat as a mirror
of silvery,
imperceptible waves.

From where I stood,
squinting in the sun,
I saw not sea
but firmament

replete with pelicans.
Two lovers bathing
stood waist-deep in clouds
and splashed themselves

with heaven. Several
yards out, in their dinghies,
the men were rapt, casting
either nets or ashes.

Women in the Sun

for Deena

She spends her summers in the Galveston sun
oblivious of melanoma and the premature
leathering of the flesh. The deepening creases

of their brows sparkling with clear fat
bullets of sweat, the two elderly women
detour around her, smug under the straw

of new panamas. Each secretly envies
her fullness and suppleness of muscle,
her bronze flesh covered with nothing

but a film of baby oil, crackling like fat
in a vat of sizzling lard. With one foot
in the grave, they detour around her,

their faces of white raisins wincing
as they reminisce the pallid history
of their own flesh robbed of the sun

by bonnets and long cotton dresses.
They envy the brash recklessness
of her youth sprawling her body

in the hot Galveston sun for days
and days on end, charging forever
the stark white batteries of her bones.

Lunatic

At midnight,
chest deep in the Gulf
and sober as the shell
of a lightning whelk,
he revels
in the misdemeanor
of his nudity.
With the velvet
hammers of his breath,

he breaks open
the geodes of minutes
and dazzles
his mildly
burning eyes.
The Gulf and the moon
lather his flesh
with creamy light,
bestowing him

with the glow
of something holy.
Hidden discreetly
in the dunes
and crumpled
beside his sandals,
lies the vulgar
sanity
of his rags.

Silverwork

A few hundred feet landward
from the seawall's a nursing home.
Late one night, by a fluke,
a patient with Alzheimer's
slipped through the front door,
clad in a blue gown and barefoot.
As she eased into the Gulf,
her gown rippled about her
like the body of a jellyfish.
An hour or so later,
they found her standing
in seawater suffused with moonglow,
staring at a school of mullet
propelling their bodies up
and out of the water,
twisting in the moonlight
like flipped silver coins, each dazzling
the unforgiving darkness
with a flash of recognition
so fleeting it slid right through
her groping, outstretched hands.

IV.

A Short Distance from the Border

Stray Bitch

Her muzzle is a shrine of scars.
Nights, she slinks in the shadows
of dumpsters, seeking a piece of eaten chicken
or bits of noodles riveted like barnacles

to the razor-edged lids of tin cans.
For years she has lived like this,
scrounging for food, keeping her distance
from cruel children, napping as she can

in the crawl space of deserted shacks.
A sister of the elements, she walks
the darkened streets, snarling at strangers,
backing into the shadows a ravaged,

unwieldy body bloated with yet another
litter of puppies, baring yellow fangs,
scorching the earth with the glorious
nipples of her loose, pendulous teats.

The Tattoo Artist

practices his craft
in deliberate
human injury
on small canvases
of clean flesh

his bloody
violent craft
which he
with his vivid inks
and needles
can only
set in motion
for a body
to complete:

a body
with its single
implement
of miracle
turning scab
and mild fever
into rose.

The Parlor

As he rides
a full moon
bleeds to death
in the morning sky.
The morning mist sizzles
on the hot pipes
of his Harley.
He kills the big engine
at the parlor
and listens
to it crack, cooling.
In the bright light
of the parlor
he gives the artist
the soft material
of his body.
He closes his eyes
and dares not move.
He leaves the parlor
feeling the big eagle
ruffling its feathers
in his back's flesh.
In the black shade
of his sleeveless shirt
he feels it
already working
its hooked beak, talons,
its dark bleeding wings.

In the Icehouse

In the lurid
neon light
of *Budweiser*
longnecks sweat
like wired
exotic dancers.
They sit
at their own table,
the fiery pulse
of double pistons
still beating
its lean drums
of thigh, buttock.
Each black wallet
is chained
to a belt loop.
They tap
their heavy skull rings
on the clean
plastic tabletop.
Boot chains glitter
in suffused hues
of red and blue.
Even the music
on the jukebox
each plays in turn
is nothing
but heavy metal.

Each a Wingless Black Angel

They don
black goggles
and rev up
the terrible engines

of their Harleys,
perched in the dark
like great gray owls
electric with dreams

of perfect murders.
They navigate
with ease
the huge black shadows

the law casts.
Deep blue nudes
shudder in the moonburned flesh
of biceps

as they gulp down
their fresh fat tablets
of speed.
They navigate

the shades of night
each a wingless
black angel
of sheer acceleration.

Campo Santo, Van Horn, Texas

Flowers of plastic
are bleached colorless
by the sun. The wind
with nothing to stop it

razes the earth
like the blades
of bulldozers
at full throttle,

leaving it
the color of dried blood.
At high noon
crosses of crude iron

cast black shadows,
shading scorpions.
Mountains
robed with rocks and cacti

ring this finished place
where bleakness reigns supreme
and only the cemetery
is growing.

Near Sundown

we sit on the west rim of the canyon
and dangle our legs in the lavender
shadow of abyss. The east canyon wall

is sunstruck, silent. We drop our eyes
to the canyon floor and fix them
on the line where sun and shadow meet.

As the stark line inches upward,
our eyes follow like the cramped fingers
of a climber pulling his body

slowly through the layered slabs
of millions of years of time,
straining for the light, pulling his body

slowly up the canyon wall
to the breathless, wind-razed fury
of the now.

For the Words

Joaquin lies still
in the black
of night.
His eyes
are swollen shut
and his body
floats in the strains
of a bleak
new music.
Moving,
he stokes the fires
of fresh cuts
and rubs bruises
looming in flesh
like blue tumors.
He can't sleep
for the words,
the proud, scarce words
of a father
telling him
again, again
how good and clean
his fight was,
how skillfully
he drew first blood.

The Goat

hangs from a heavy branch
by its hind hooves.
Morning's dawn-blushed
and tainted with the peals
of distant iron bells.
The goat's throat cut
Jesus catches
a cup of hot blood
and drinks it.
The goat dies
with its eyes wide-open
as if watching
the earth's rapt acceptance
of its offering.
Jesus sharpens his knife
for the skinning
and feels the bright hot life
settling in his belly.

Of Crows and Cornfields

The fields
are shining seas
teeming with stalks
of corn dead as straw.

The wind
is stirring them
with the sound of beetles
gnawing dry wood.

The dusk
is parchment,
a sheet of a score
of music,

the power lines
a staff
on which
whole notes

of crows
are ever so
masterfully
riveted.

Their Meek Provisions

As if by choice
they keep the soles
of their sandals wafer-thin
narrowing the distance

between their flesh
and the sun-baked earth
of late August
and they clutch

their meek provisions
of meal, limes, and dried black beans,
stopping now and then
for red lights,

their sterling Christs
chained about their necks, sliding
down the warm dark cleavage
of their breasts.

Madonna and Child

The cathedral rises from the earth
like the sheer rock face of a mountain.
From its lofty perch in the belfry,
the raven gazes at the beggar

on the street below. She is kneeling,
covered completely by her black cloak,
reaching through a fold her cupped,
clawed hand, lifeless as a wooden ladle.

With what dignity she begs,
uttering not a word, nodding her thanks
in utter darkness for a single *peso*.
She'll stay this way for hours in the sun,

making under her cloak the sign of the cross
to each passerby, praying in silence
for that most blessed of His miracles
turning meal into milk

for the toothless gums of her infant.
As she prays the raven shudders,
ruffling its feathers, ringing the bells
of their elegant darkness.

The Light of Mexico

It's no wonder the painters
love it so; the way,
in little villages,
it brings out the pinks, greens,

blues, yellows, and lavenders
of humble houses
dazzling the flanks of mountains
like strewn fruit; the way,

at zero hour, suits of it
mesmerize the eyes of bulls;
the way, as if from nowhere,
it sparkles the dark,

chocolate eyes of mothers
so comfortable with death
they candy its skulls
for the tongues of bronze children.

El Camino del Rio

Low-water crossings,
loose livestock, steep grades
and sharp curves are common
along this scenic drive
beside the Rio Grande
between Lajitas and Presidio.

The river, patient
as a sedulous sculptor
spellbound for thousands of years
by his work, employing
his single utensil of water,
has carved walls of stone

towering hundreds of feet.
The Apaches knew them
as the places of no return. Only
the screams of hawks, bouncing
ad infinitum off the canyon walls,
sound as if they belong.

(photo of Larry Thomas by Jan Moore)

Born and raised in West Texas, Larry D. Thomas earned his B.A. degree in English from the University of Houston. In 1998, he retired from a career in adult criminal justice with the Harris County, Texas, Community Supervision and Corrections Department, where he served as a branch manager from 1983-1998. Book-length manuscripts of Thomas' poetry were selected as finalists in the 1993 and 1997 Southern and Southwestern Poets Breakthrough Series competitions sponsored by *Texas Review* Press and the Summer 2000 Pecan Grove Press national chapbook competition. His poetry and reviews have appeared in numerous national journals, including the *Southwest Review*, *Poet Lore*, *The Midwest Quarterly*, *The Texas Review*, *Borderlands: Texas Poetry Review*, *The Spoon River Poetry Review*, *Cottonwood*, *The Journal of the American Medical Association*, *Puerto del Sol*, *Writers' Forum*, *The Chattahoochee Review*, *International Poetry Review*, *The Cape Rock* and *Louisiana Literature*.